ANCIENT CIVILIZATIONS Need to Know

SilverTip

The Rise and Fall of Ancient Egypt

by D. R. Faust

Consultant: Caitlin Krieck, Social Studies Teacher and Instructional Coach, The Lab School of Washington

BEARPORT
PUBLISHING

Minneapolis, Minnesota

Credits

Cover and title page, © givaga/Shutterstock; 5, © mountainpix/Shutterstock; 7, © Tasawer/Shutterstock; 9, © Art Berry/Shutterstock; 10, © Chronicle/Alamy Stock Photo; 11, © Ivan Moreno sl/Shutterstock; 13, © robertharding/Alamy Stock Photo; 15, © FORGET Patrick/Alamy Stock Photo; 16–17, © TwoDeeGraphix/Shutterstock; 19, © AMIR MAKAR/Getty Images; 21T, © MET/BOT/Alamy Stock Photo; 21B, © MET/BOT/Alamy Stock Photo; 23, © PRISMA ARCHIVO/Alamy Stock Photo; 25, © Universal History Archive /Getty Images; 27, © Apic /Getty Images; 28a, © Chronicle/Alamy Stock Photo; 28b, © FORGET Patrick/Alamy Stock Photo; 28c, © AMIR MAKAR/Getty Images; 28d, © PRISMA ARCHIVO/Alamy Stock Photo; 28e, © Curioso.Photography/Shutterstock.

Bearport Publishing Company Product Development Team

President: Jen Jenson; Director of Product Development: Spencer Brinker; Managing Editor: Allison Juda; Associate Editor: Naomi Reich; Associate Editor: Tiana Tran; Art Director: Colin O'Dea; Designer: Kim Jones; Designer: Kayla Eggert; Product Development Assistant: Owen Hamlin

Statement on Usage of Generative Artificial Intelligence

Bearport Publishing remains committed to publishing high-quality nonfiction books. Therefore, we restrict the use of generative AI to ensure accuracy of all text and visual components pertaining to a book's subject. See BearportPublishing.com for details.

A Note on Colorization

Some of the historic photos in this book have been colorized to help readers have a more meaningful and rich experience. The color results are not intended to depict actual historical detail.

Library of Congress Cataloging-in-Publication Data

Names: Faust, Daniel R., author.
Title: The rise and fall of ancient Egypt / by D. R. Faust.
Other titles: Ancient civilizations (Minneapolis, Minn.)
Description: Silvertip books. | Minneapolis, Minnesota : Bearport
  Publishing Company, [2025] | Series: Ancient civilizations: need to know
  | Includes bibliographical references and index.
Identifiers: LCCN 2023059750 (print) | LCCN 2023059751 (ebook) | ISBN
  9798892320436 (library binding) | ISBN 9798892325172 (paperback) | ISBN
  9798892321761 (ebook)
Subjects: LCSH: Egypt—History—To 640 A.D. | Egypt—Civilization.
Classification: LCC DT83 .F38 2025 (print) | LCC DT83 (ebook) | DDC
  932—dc23/eng/20240130
LC record available at https://lccn.loc.gov/2023059750
LC ebook record available at https://lccn.loc.gov/2023059751

Copyright © 2025 Bearport Publishing Company. All rights reserved. No part of this publication may be reproduced in whole or in part, stored in any retrieval system, or transmitted in any form or by any means, electronic, mechanical, photocopying, recording, or otherwise, without written permission from the publisher. Bearport Publishing is a division of Chrysalis Education Group.

For more information, write to Bearport Publishing, 5357 Penn Avenue South, Minneapolis, MN 55419.

Contents

Old but Not Forgotten 4
A River in Egypt. 6
Two Egypts Become One 8
Dynasties Rule. 12
The Age of Pyramids. 14
Divided and Reunited. 18
The Egyptian Empire 22
Rediscovering the Past. 26

Ancient Egypt Timeline 28
SilverTips for Success 29
Glossary .30
Read More 31
Learn More Online 31
Index 32
About the Author 32

Old but Not Forgotten

You've probably heard of Egypt's pyramids. And most people have come across stories of mummies. You may even know about some famous **pharaohs**. But did you know these things came from one of the oldest **civilizations** on Earth?

Modern Egypt is a country in northeast Africa. Ancient Egypt was in the same part of the world. But life back then was very different.

A River in Egypt

Much of Egypt is covered in harsh desert. The Nile River provides some of the only relief from the dry heat. So, when people first settled the area, they lived along the Nile. It gave them water for drinking. The soil along the river was good for farming.

> The land around the Nile is known as the Nile valley. At its northern end, the river spreads out into **wetlands**. It forms a triangular **delta**. Here, the Nile drains into the Mediterranean Sea.

Two Egypts Become One

Ancient Egypt was divided into two parts. Lower Egypt was located in the north. This region had **fertile** wetlands. Upper Egypt was in the drier lands to the south.

Each of these areas was also broken into smaller states. Many may have had their own kings or governments.

> Why was Lower Egypt north and Upper Egypt south? It has to do with the movement of the Nile. Unlike most rivers, the Nile flows from south to north.

In 3100 BCE, the two Egypts were united under a single king. This started an era known as the early dynastic period. During this time, we see the first written records of the region. They marked the passage of time based on rulers.

Some records say Egypt's first king was Menes. Others claim it was Narmer. There are some people who think Menes and Narmer were the same person. We may never know the truth.

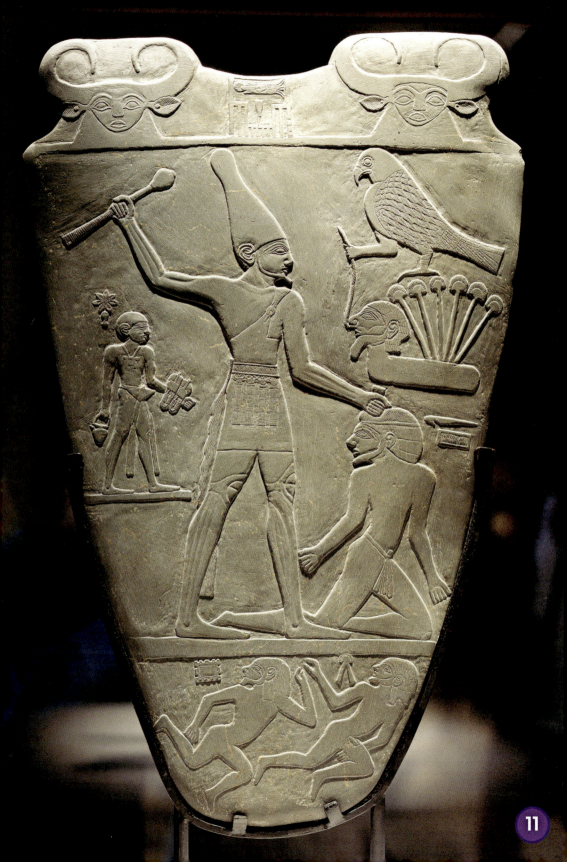

Dynasties Rule

The dynastic period gets its name from the way the civilization was ruled. Ancient Egypt was run by a series of **dynasties**. A line of leaders from the same family would rule for a long time. Then, another family would gain control. This new dynasty would lead the civilization for a while.

> Kings in ancient Egypt were often treated as godlike. Egyptians believed kings connected the people with the gods. These leaders were very powerful.

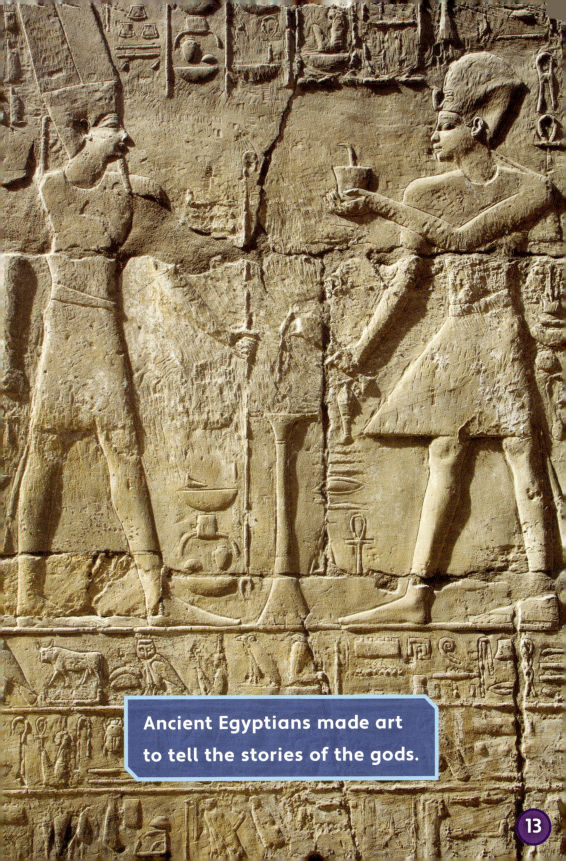
Ancient Egyptians made art to tell the stories of the gods.

The Age of Pyramids

The power of ancient Egypt grew. The civilization entered a time called the Old Kingdom. This era lasted from around 2650 to 2150 BCE. It was considered the first of three great kingdoms, or periods, of ancient Egyptian history. Kings from this time made strong central governments.

> Some consider Djoser to be the first king of the Old Kingdom. He was part of Egypt's third dynasty. Djoser ruled from the capital city of Memphis. He was the first king buried in a pyramid.

King Djoser

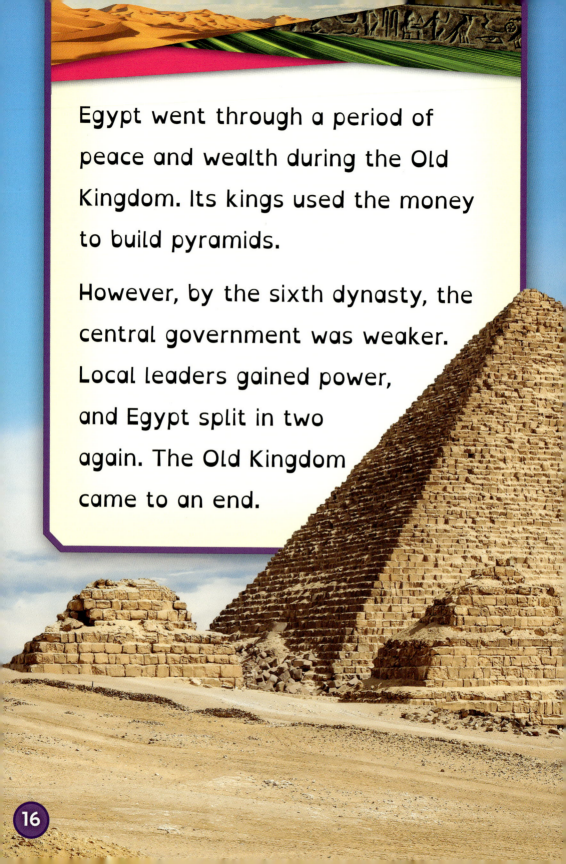

Egypt went through a period of peace and wealth during the Old Kingdom. Its kings used the money to build pyramids.

However, by the sixth dynasty, the central government was weaker. Local leaders gained power, and Egypt split in two again. The Old Kingdom came to an end.

The Old Kingdom is often called the Age of the Pyramid Builders. Egyptian rulers had many pyramids built during the third and fourth dynasties. They were made as burial chambers for the kings.

Divided and Reunited

Each of ancient Egypt's three kingdoms was followed by an **intermediate** period. During the First Intermediate period, Upper and Lower Egypt fought.

By about 1968 BCE, 11th dynasty ruler Mentuhotep II took power. He reunited Egypt, ushering in the Middle Kingdom.

> Thebes became Egypt's capital during part of this time. The city was split by the Nile. The main part was on the east bank. The west side had many tombs and temples built for the dead.

The Middle Kingdom is known for its beautiful art and writing. The rulers of the 12th dynasty expanded the civilization. There was, once again, stability.

This era ended when part of northern Egypt broke away. The Second Intermediate period started about 1630 BCE.

> The Middle Kingdom saw the Classical Age of ancient Egypt. Many believe this is when the civilization's art and culture reached its peak.

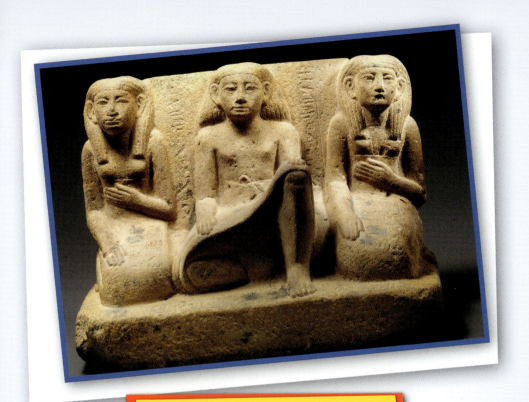

Art and writing from the Middle Kingdom

The Egyptian Empire

The New Kingdom formed under the first king of the 18th dynasty. Ahmose I reunited Egypt around 1540 BCE.

The New Kingdom had a new wave of growth. Its leaders took over lands to the south and east. Trade with other groups brought in even more wealth.

> Egypt's rulers were long called kings and queens. During the New Kingdom, the titles changed. The leaders became pharaohs.

Ahmose I

As the civilization grew, Egypt faced threats. Outsiders tried to **invade**. The fighting increased, and Egypt became weaker. It broke apart once more. This marked the start of the Third Intermediate period. It would be ancient Egypt's last era.

Bit by bit, Egypt fell. After thousands of years, Egypt no longer ruled itself.

> The Kush fought over part of ancient Egypt. In 671 BCE, Assyrians invaded. Then, in 332 BCE, Alexander the Great of Greece came. Egypt was part of the Roman Empire within 300 years.

Rediscovering the Past

The ancient Egyptian civilization was rediscovered during the 1800s. Britain and France fought in the region. As they battled, these European powers began to explore. They learned more about the art and culture of ancient Egypt. This brought new interest to the region's past.

Howard Carter found King Tut's tomb in 1922. It was filled with art, furniture, and weapons. News of this discovery spread. It made ancient Egypt more popular than ever.

Howard Carter with King Tut's sarcophagus

Ancient Egypt Timeline

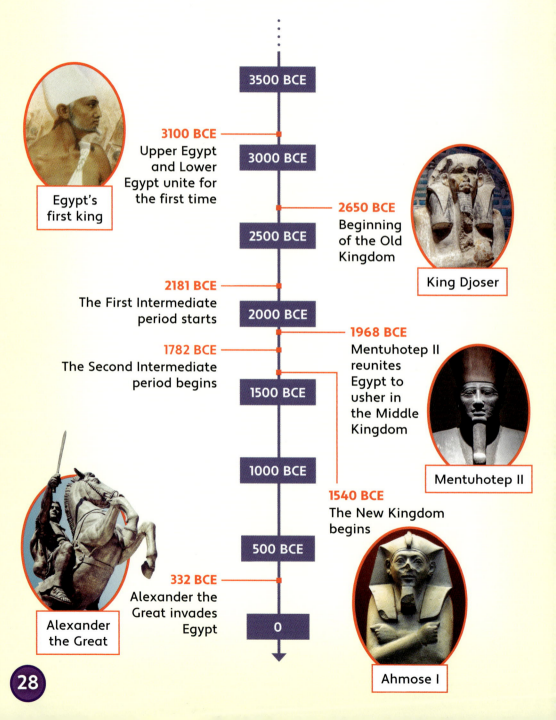

SilverTips for SUCCESS

★ SilverTips for REVIEW

Review what you've learned. Use the text to help you.

Define key terms

dynasties
Middle Kingdom
New Kingdom
Nile River
Old Kingdom

Check for understanding

What role did the Nile play in the growth of ancient Egypt?

How are the different periods of ancient Egyptian history divided?

What led to the ultimate fall of the power of ancient Egypt?

Think deeper

Explain which period of ancient Egyptian history you think was the most influential.

★ SilverTips on TEST-TAKING

- **Make a study plan.** Ask your teacher what the test is going to cover. Then, set aside time to study a little bit every day.

- **Read all the questions carefully.** Be sure you know what is being asked.

- **Skip any questions** you don't know how to answer right away. Mark them and come back later if you have time.

Glossary

civilizations large groups of people who share the same history and way of life

delta a piece of land shaped like a triangle that forms where a river splits into smaller rivers before flowing into an ocean or sea

dynasties groups of rulers from the same family whose periods of control over ancient Egypt mark the passage of time

fertile able to help plants grow

intermediate being or happening in the middle

invade to take over a place by force

pharaohs rulers of ancient Egypt from the New Kingdom or later

wetlands swampy areas near lakes and rivers

Read More

Jopp, Kelsey. *Giza Pyramids (Structural Wonders).* Lake Elmo, MN: Focus Readers, 2023.

Mather, Charis. *The Peculiar Past in Ancient Egypt (Strange History).* Minneapolis: Bearport Publishing Company, 2024.

Quick, Megan. *How Did Kids Live in Ancient Egypt? (Kids in History).* Buffalo, NY: Gareth Stevens Publishing, 2024.

Learn More Online

1. Go to **www.factsurfer.com** or scan the QR code below.
2. Enter "**Civilizations Ancient Egypt**" into the search box.
3. Click on the cover of this book to see a list of websites.

Index

art 13, 20–21, 26

dynasties 12, 14, 16–18, 20, 22

early dynastic period 10, 12

intermediate periods 18, 20, 24, 28

invaders 24

kings 8, 10, 12, 14–17, 22, 26–28

Lower Egypt 8–9, 18, 28

Middle Kingdom, the 18, 20–21, 28

New Kingdom, the 22, 28

Nile River 6–9, 18

Old Kingdom, the 14, 16–17, 28

pharaohs 4, 22

pyramids 4, 14, 16–17

Upper Egypt 8–9, 18, 28

writing 10, 20–21

About the Author

D. R. Faust is a freelance writer of fiction and nonfiction. They live in Queens, NY.